DAD,

The Man

The Myth

The Legend

By C. Lawrence Desmore

Copyright © 2016
Bethune Publishing – The Bethune Group
Clayton L. Desmore
a/k/a C. Lawrence Desmore First Printing
All rights reserved, including the right
to reproduce this work in any form whatsoever
without written permission from the publisher,
except for brief passages in connection with a
review.
Photographs may not be reproduced without
permission of the owner.
For information write: Bethune
Publishing, Inc.
P. O. Box 2008
Daytona Beach, FL 2115-2008
docbethune@tbginc.org Phone: 386-999-0092

Cover designed by **John-Mark McLeod**
J2maginations, LLC J2maginations@gmail.com

Book design and page layout by Bethune
Publishing, Inc.

Printed in the United States of America Library
of Congress Control Number: 2016921289
ISBN 978-1946566010

Table of Contents

Contents   *Page #*

From Lucy with Love	1
Foreword	2
Prologue	5
A Letter to my Dad – Corey	7
A City Boy Growing Up in a Rural Area	9
Four Months Before My Senior Year	12
Round Two of the Last Year in Senior High	39
First Time in the Navy	47
The Vietnam War	55
Life at Daytona Beach Community College (DBCC)	70
The Gates	81
Years Later	89
Leaving DBCC	92
The Year 2002	97
Hello Daddy	107
Laying the Headstone	112

DAD, THE MAN, THE MYTH, THE LEGEND
C. LAWRENCE DESMORE

Clayton:

This book reveals your dedication and determination. Your words elevate so many minds; your young and old. It is my hope that you will continue to write. You have a second book waiting for birth from this master piece alone. After you complete the sequel, move on to the other inspirational thoughts for more books…we are thirsty for your true gift.

It is a gift to provide our young men and women with a challenge and encouragement! I am EXTREMELY proud of you.

Your loving wife

Lucy

Foreword

The Man, The Myth, The Legend

Definitions:

The Man: Adam, used as the proper name of the first man. The name is derived from a word meaning "to be red," and thus the first man was called Adam because he was formed from the red earth. It is also the generic name of the human race (Genesis 1:26 Genesis 1:27 ; 5:2 ; 8:21 ; Deuteronomy 8:3).v

The Myth: a traditional or legendary story, usually concerning some being or hero or event, with or without a determinable basis of fact or a natural explanation, especially one that is concerned with deities or demigods and explains some practice, rite, or phenomenon of nature.

The Legend: a story coming down from the past.

Clayton Desmore has taken these three words to craft a story of historical nature and factual significance. He has managed to weave a tale of honest projection of his life seen through his eyes and the eyes of others, but manipulated by time. Time manipulation--in the era that Mr. Desmore grew up there was such drastic change in American history that just keeping up with the *Tsunami* called change was difficult but was captured in his book by circumstances he was personally involved in or had witnessed.

This book is also a history lesson for people who have grown up in an era of assimilation and have never witnessed or read about how it was before the assimilation of Blacks into the public-school system. Clayton walked down memory lane and has given us a clear poetic picture of historical times. It can be used as a blueprint for coming of age...boy, man, fatherhood, husband and friend.

It is with pleasure that I decided to take the trip down Mr. Desmore's lane of honesty unsurpassed and read how his journey was a life lesson not only for his children, but for others as well. Congratulations on your first life lesson book that people will enjoy now and in the future.

Donna Gray-Banks

Founder and Director

Fresh Book Festival – Daytona Beach, FL

PROLOGUE

This book is a collection of stories about the life of C. Lawrence Desmore that I wish to share with my children.

These stories are experiences I have lived that we've never talked about. However, you need to know that your father is human and has made mistakes and here are some of them. The difference between success and defeat, is **how you handle it**. If you can look at yourself tomorrow and vow that you learned from yesterday's mistakes, then you can say;

THIS WILL NEVER HAPPEN A-G-A-I-N!

This is twenty plus years of learning. Some lessons have been negative and some very positive. But all in all, it was life. Sometimes the wait is worth it, I only hope you, my children and other readers enjoy it.

DAD, "THE MAN, THE MYTH, THE LEGEND"

DAD, THE MAN, THE MYTH, THE LEGEND
C. LAWRENCE DESMORE

December 5, 1995

Daddy,

How do you convince a parent that he has done a good job in raising his kids? What do you give a parent that cares so deeply about his sons that he would fight for their custody in court?

What is the best possible way to congratulate the man that gave me life, a home, a helping hand whenever I was in distress and lots of love to live on? Such a man as this (Daddy) is known to be a legend in the history of parenthood. I cannot think of a time that I really needed you and you weren't there.

You've watched me grow from a baby into a man. I heard you tell me at times that you have never been a father before, but you could have fooled me.

I'm writing this letter to you to let you know how much I love and appreciate you, being my father and best friend throughout the years. Nicky and I are very blessed to have you as a father. I am going to miss you and Nicky while I am up north in boot camp. I plan to call you from Jacksonville when I settle into my room. Give the rest of the family my love!!

Don't forget!

I'm proud of you for getting me this far. You are the wind beneath my wings.

Love,

Corey Desmore

A CITY BOY GROWING UP IN A RURAL AREA

DAD, THE MAN, THE MYTH, THE LEGEND
C. LAWRENCE DESMORE

We moved to Santos, Florida when I was in the 8th grade. I had my first musical challenge in band, with a girl in the 11th grade. She was really good. I **had** to practice every night and on weekends and she would practice with me. I think she was my first crush and love affair.

When I was having some problem in Science class, she was there to help with that. I did not enjoy seeing her graduate and leave for college. When I reached the 10th grade all males were required to take agriculture classes for the two remaining years.

The agriculture teacher knew of me, but did not know what a clown I could be. The State Fair started in February. The first week is devoted to FFA (Future Farmers of America) and FHA (Future Homemaker of America).

Our group didn't have enough guys so they asked me to go as an alternate. On the way to the fair we had two flat tires and no jack. The teacher told us to get out of the truck and lift it, then asked me to slide the spare on (I was the smallest person). As they lifted the truck, I thought of a joke and started to tell it. Everybody let the truck go but the teacher. He was so furious, he cursed me out bad.

We went on to the fair. I didn't know a rooster from a hen, or a bull from a cow, I was so bad the teacher said to me "go walk around' until we were through, and I did. It was then I began to enjoy the fair fully. I met up with this girl that I had met in Daytona last summer and we walked around together.

The time came to head back home; and we, unfortunately, had another flat tire. The service station was about a mile away so the teacher went to get the tire patched, and we went to a Strip Club that was a few blocks away. When he returned, we were gone, so he took a nap while waiting for us.

He chewed us out the entire way home. I was never asked to go to another FFA judging contest again.

FOUR MONTHS BEFORE MY SENIOR YEAR

DAD, THE MAN, THE MYTH, THE LEGEND
C. LAWRENCE DESMORE

January 1968 was as usual; Christmas break was over and ahead was the last half of the school year. I was very happy because this was the time that when we began campaigning for SGA (Student Government Association) officers. I was popular and smart enough to win the President's position.

With the campaign in full swing in March we learned that our school was to be phased out. **Integration**. If you lived in this area you went to a school 12 miles north and my new school is 15 miles south.

The principal at the "new school" visited our campus to talk with students in the south area. This speech was the first time someone ever lied to me with so much sincerity. Remember, I was seventeen, active in church and honest. I couldn't lie if I wanted too. In the speech, I remember him saying there were four black students, one Indian student (Joe) and 322 white students. "All 85 of you will be welcomed."

All hell broke loose after that meeting. One

of my female classmates cut a senior female (dating the same guy). It was ugly and we were upset to the point of war because we wouldn't graduate together. This change separated sweethearts, cousins and friends. One of my friends hit this principal with a rock. We cracked up and spent the afternoon in our principal's office.

Mr. Hart, our principal, quickly shared his feelings because his job was unclear, but we sat trying to think of what would happen next. As I write this, I'm wrapped in thoughts of my class reunion in August 1994, the first official one, some twenty-five years a f t e r
graduation. Oh, how we sang our school's Alma Mater that my Dad wrote. What happened to our records, awards...does anyone know or even care?

We were handcuffed. It wasn't anything we could do to stop integration. "The beginning of an ended era." Even today, I ponder the rational of integration. How can it be such a great plan when

DAD, THE MAN, THE MYTH, THE LEGEND
C. LAWRENCE DESMORE

I'm not Colored or a Negro, but an African-American male that pays taxes and still is treated as an invisible part of this great nation? My opinion on integration is that the gain for African-Americans was exposure to many injustices and White Americas still don't want to right this wrong.

April 4, 1968, was the second time in my short life I witnessed a nation in panic. The first time was the assignation of President John F. Kennedy in 1963.

The flag was lowered, the principal announced over the public-address system "the President has been shot", God bless America was played, then he dismissed school for the day.
Mom worked for some white folks and she came home early. Everybody was crying. At that time, Presidents in this country were saints. That is up until the Nixon era.

The Kennedy's were OK with us because they worked with our leader Dr. Martin Luther King, Jr., which brings me back to April 4, 1968.

DAD, THE MAN, THE MYTH, THE LEGEND
C. LAWRENCE DESMORE

This was the most puzzled day of my life; our leader assassinated by James Earl Ray. I didn't know what to think. I felt bitter but Dr. King taught us that violence would lead to more death and that it will happen anyway. So, keep the movement alive.

My "present" principal earlier asked student leaders to meet weekly to talk with the younger students that would attend the "new school" next year to minimize problems. The meeting that week was at my house. We reviewed the promises the two principals made. No elections for Student Government officers until we arrived. Student council will vote with activities advisors making sure we were included if we were interested.

We would have equal treatment with my group, I chose my girlfriend and two captains in each of the lower grades. The captains played a very important role because if anything happened they could explain the truth to their peers and if we had to take action they knew why. My girlfriend's job was equally important as a captain with two exceptions. First, be my extra eyes and ears and second, help me plan because next year she would lead.

Graduation day at our black school was a bittersweet occasion; the graduating seniors dedicated their last program to us. The bitter part was I had only lived in this town five years, my Dad wanted me to come home to Daytona to prepare my life for college and I felt compelled to stay and fight for the movement. My friends trusted my judgment and I was not going to leave them now. I also felt Mom wanted to see how my friends and I would handle it.

Knowing I would never let my parents down, although we may not always agree, but usually after discussion things were okay. I think parents do this to see how well thought out their children's plans are.

Summer ended, we returned to the city of Belleview two weeks before school started. Sometime that summer we received letters (my sisters, brothers and myself) indicating what bus to catch and when and where to report to once we arrived. We had to wake up two hours earlier to catch the bus for what seemed to be a one-hour ride to school (thank God, I could drive).

Knowing I only needed one class "Problems of American Democracy", Dad and Mom made sure we took more classes than needed. Earlier we attended Summer School because it kept us off the streets. "Son, this is why I sent you to Summer School."

Take a deep breath and join me on my first day at my fourth school and the first one with white teachers and students. As the six orange "blue bird" buses approached the high school, everyone's eyes were as big as they could be, looking out the windows at the school, parking lots and surroundings.

There were no "Welcome Mats", only the principal, his African-American assistant principal and a few students walking around staring at us as we arrived.

DAD, THE MAN, THE MYTH, THE LEGEND
C. LAWRENCE DESMORE

The bus stopped to unload. Of course, the principal was compelled to let us know who was in charge. The speech was short, with instructions on where our homerooms were and that assembly was at 10:30 a.m.

At this point, everything was okay with his first move; of course, I had made my move before we got there. It was to avoid problems (name calling). No one should be alone, buddy up. Overnight we would have a voice at this school.

On my way to homeroom, I met with some old classmates I hadn't seen over the summer, and met with new classmates from another school that were placed here. In my homeroom class, the environment was typical. Friends sat with friends, which created the division of the races that would make or break this school.

Oddly, the homeroom teacher instructed the class that I needed to graduate. As she called roll some of the white students needed every letter in the alphabet to spell their names, whereas today, some African-Americans would not know how to pronounce theirs before the fifth birthday or spell it before the sixth. We joked at some classmates, trying to remember their names and faces, after all isn't humor everlasting?

Well, "*Ms. Thang*" let us know it wasn't funny, thinking everyone was probably laughing at her. Everyone had his or her schedules. I had Typing, Art, Band, Home Economics and Drama, and PAD (Problems of American Democracy), the only class I need to graduate.

The bell rang, time for assembly. The principal stood at the podium greeting the teachers and students with a welcome. His agenda was, seniors would enter all assemblies last, sit up front, and exit first. I felt pleased with his statement because it's no easy task becoming a senior in a rural area and Lord knows I've been in so many bands (6) and schools (4) that I was very ready to graduate. The next comment almost caused a riot. He introduced the Student

Government officers and I walked out. The other black students followed. I was mad, he was mad, and the white students knew something was wrong, but apparently, no one knew about his promise on the elections.

This action set the tone for my trust in him. He knew I was dead serious about my belief and trust. I learned that first day of the power I had when the students walked out with me. I loved that moment.

Once outside, a few of my classmates came to show support before my girlfriend and the captains got there. The big question was what are they going to do with us? I paused then answered. "They can't do anything yet, and they can't do anything to all of us". By that time, the assistant principal came over to talk with me, alone. Okay cool.

We went to his office, he sent for my folder. As we waited, he shared his views of what happened. I listened thinking why didn't he ask me about my action? Well the folder arrived; he looked over it checking to see if he knew my parents and ask for my parent's phone number to keep in his pocket. That's when I realize he should be on my team. Well, the principal sent for me and I asked the assistant to come with me, he did, which surprised the principal. I began to explain my action and if any punishment was to be given it should start and end with me, although he knew he had lied.

He didn't apologize but offered a compromise. He said, "the election will stand" but this year we will have two Student Government Groups, one black, one white with equal members and equal votes and meetings will be shared. My heart was racing I couldn't wait to tell everyone what had happened. Is this okay with you Mr. Desmore? I answered, "Yes" with my big smile, then asking when do we vote, he said "all the black students will assemble again today to vote."

I was glad to leave that office because the other students needed to know what was happening before something happened for real.

DAD, THE MAN, THE MYTH, THE LEGEND
C. LAWRENCE DESMORE

The announcement was made. We gathered in the auditorium. The principal asked us to stay until he finished explaining the SGA plan for 1969. He suggested that I be President of the black student group. Everybody stood clapping and cheering. I wanted to cry, because that's what I wanted.

I didn't know why he suggested me. Maybe it's because I would probably be in his office everyday anyway, or had he looked at my folder. Remember, this was my fourth school. Was it my leadership in the band or maybe the way I spoke up in his office? I took the podium, looked at him and told him about my staff (my girlfriend and the captains) and they would pick the positions they wanted and that two additional seniors and one junior will be voted to this board.

He was shocked at how well thought out our plans were. The assistant principal saluted with the right-on power sign.

What a morning; we had lunch, toured the campus and met with teachers. We could not meet with the Student Government body because of the earlier walkout and he hadn't discussed the new plan with the white students.

The first SGA meeting was Friday, so he had time to inform them. Those of us that were interested in other activities such as football, cheerleading, basketball and band attended those meetings.

My area was band, we met the director of music, and he announced class and practice hours. I sensed he had never worked with African- American musicians, because I didn't know him. Remember, my Dad is a music instructor and I had never heard of him. I noticed a folder of music on a stand, marches and concerts but no popular music. Seemed like another challenge to meet with tomorrow. What a day.

Mom asked us about the first day at school. After my sisters and brother talked I shared my day. Everyone went "what", it's only the first day. The next couple of days were okay. We attended classes still finding our way around. In band practice, we retained our current seats (I played cornet solo chair). I knew this band instructor was glad we were there, the size grew by 50% and the volume by 500%, we really could play. Some weekends my brother and I would play with my Dad's school band.

Music was third in our family, only behind religion and family, and family wasn't just in our home, it was community as well. If someone needed something you were there. I remember a man was run over by his tractor. He could not work his farm and get produce to market. So, after school a group of us would work for him although he never asked.

At SGA meeting the white students were upset and that was expected. It was decided that the white students conduct the first meeting and we would have every other one. Imagine ordering uniforms (football, cheer-leader, band, and basketball, etc.) this late. The football team voted to dress the best players. I think the cheer-leaders made their uniforms and the band waited on the orders. We didn't perform on the field the first two games, but we practiced the routines. It appeared that things were Okay... not by a long shot.

One afternoon at band practice we opened our music folders; this was the biggest mistake the band director could have made. The music for "Dixie" was there. Can you picture me playing Dixie? I asked if he was serious. His response was "yes". I quietly put my horn back in its case and went straight to the principal's office. The assistant principal saw me with my horn case and asked what is the problem?

As I explained that "I do not play any damn Dixie for no one". About that time all the black students were at the office and very loud. It was good it was after school. They put me out of the office and called for the band director. The three talked and then came out and said Dixie would not be played, then we went back to practice. I was making them white folks mad at me and I was gaining more respect. I wasn't being mean, but what I felt was right. What do I look like or why would I want to play something about slavery and picking cotton? I think he thought no one would react this way, but I had no choice.

Word quickly spread about this. People called my home thanking me, or cursing my family and me, but my friends were there for me. Shortly after the incident my homeroom and PAD teacher said the Black Power Fist was Communist. I told her that I had never seen or heard of a Black Communist, only white folk were and the local group was the KKK (Ku Klux Klan). She yelled, "You go to", I interrupted smartly, "I'm going, where's my hall pass"? On my way to the principal's office I thought maybe I should have a desk in his office. Well Mr. Desmore, what have you done now? (Like who have you pissed off)? He told me "two afternoons of detention", I said, "what about her?" He snapped back "you are suspended for two days".

I thought my Mom would kill me, but she knew I would stand up for my beliefs. My classmates got the assignments and I chilled at home, unlike the times you got suspended for fighting and I made you go the library to research and write a paper on Black History.

Shortly after returning my next big event was Homecoming. Surprisingly some whites under-stood what I was trying to do and asked if they could help. One girl and I became good school friends and some of the guys in the band and I would play football at their home or mine on the weekends. I was cautious and they understood. The school's policy on Homecoming candidates was the senior's vote on twelve contestants. We had three blacks, of the twelve; the top five would be Homecoming court and Queen. We didn't have a chance to set one with thirty-eight votes going three ways. What am I going to do?

I thought of a block vote (a write in candidate). I arranged a meeting with the captains and my girlfriend on how this would win a black queen. Next, was to convince one of the three to run. The first two I asked said no because they were scared. I didn't like it but I understood. The third classmate was one of the two black females at the school before we got there and she was very smart and delighted. Remember, the white girl I mentioned earlier found out about the plan and offered her help. I asked her to do my homework, and she did. When the Blacks found out, they were mad. Anyway, the elections were held. The SGA counted the ballots three times before telling the principal (the vote wasn't even close, but they wanted a recount).

    The principal was in an assembly waiting to announce the winner. We gave him the envelope and sat down. My heart was beating very fast. We won the block vote. Personally, I wanted the win but we needed a person of color on that court and she agreed not to be second but a queen and we delivered. He looked at the list, turned red, read it, got redder and then looked at me with those *in my office* eyes. I raised my hand and he said "yes". This time it was him and me, alone. He took his ring off and spun it on the glass top desk and it reflected KKK. He said "Mr. Desmore, you will meet with the teachers today after school to discuss your actions", and he personally wanted them to vote to suspend me from this school. "Can you understand what kind of problems you are causing? These people are adults, majority white and they don't care about you or your treatment in pass years."

He then told me that if anything happened at Homecoming when the lights go off, he would have me arrested in another county." I asked, "Why do the lights have to be off?" He thought, "well that's a good point, but if anything happens, I'm looking for you."

At the teachers meeting I was suspended for five days after the Homecoming game. There were no problems at Homecoming, however I was very visible so I was as safe as anyone could imagine. Every Black student at that school knew about this. I started driving with a gun, because I was going to be ready.

DAD, THE MAN, THE MYTH, THE LEGEND
C. LAWRENCE DESMORE

Well, Christmas was near. I was ready for the break. One might think all those days at home from being suspended, I didn't need the break, but I did because I would get calls all the time. I thought my Mom would change the phone number, which wouldn't help either.

School was finally over for Christmas. During the break your grandma let your uncle and I pick fruit (oranges, grapefruit and tangerines). I thought watermelons, peanuts and peas were hard to pick. Try fruit from trees. You must position your ladder to be at the top of the tree, sack the fruit, come down the ladder with the fruit sack, dump it in the boxes, put your ticket on the boxes and start all over again. You do this all-day long.

The first day, I picked twenty-eight boxes. I thought I had done something, about t w e n t y dollars' worth when my friends were doubling and tripling my count. I wanted to quit, but at that point I wanted to prove to myself that I could do hard physical work and be smart. You can't tell a man about hard work if you've never done it.

DAD, THE MAN, THE MYTH, THE LEGEND
C. LAWRENCE DESMORE

1933 Thru 1968

Yesteryears' Memories

Former Belleview-Santos High School

Seventh Annual Reunion Of Staff, Students and Community Souvenir Book

July 5, 2014 - 10:00 A.M. - 3:00 P.M.

Holiday Inn & Suites, Ocala
Conference Center
3600 SW 38th Ave. - Ocala, FL 34474

DAD, THE MAN, THE MYTH, THE LEGEND
C. LAWRENCE DESMORE

A Tribute to Mr. Matthew Everett Hart, Jr.
Principal 1949 - 1966

Mr. Hart became principal of Belleview-Santos in 1949. With the love, support and encouragement of his lovely wife, he guided Belleview-Santos toward its destiny. He arrived at BS, driving an old but stylish 1936 two-seated Ford. It was basic black! However, things were looking up because shortly after his arrival he bought a "brand new" 1949 Ford. Again of course, it was basic black! He also brought with him a new energy, enthusiasm and commitment to change, progress and to improvement. In response to the needs and concerns of the community he established a goal of Belleview-Santos becoming a full-fledged high school. There was not a black high school in the south end of the county. Therefore, students from Weirsdale, Summerfield, Belleview, Hopeville, Shady Grove and Santos were required to travel to Ocala in order to earn a high school diploma. He recognized this as a barrier to many of these students continuing their education beyond the junior high level. Mr. Hart used his considerable drive, determination, persuasiveness, and Machiavellian skills to cause the "powers that be" to support his vision for the school and his mission.

There was an immediate need for more space in order to expand the curriculum and programs. An existing building was relocated from Shady Grove to the Belleview-Santos campus. This building housed the home economics classes and served as the school's first cafeteria or lunchroom. A second building was moved from Jerusalem to the Belleview-Santos site. It was used to house the science and social studies classes.

Alpha — December 21, 1915
Omega — March 11, 2000

The 'Hart' years were one of tremendous anticipation, excitement, growth and accomplishments. What he could not get the County School Board to do, he often did himself with the parents, teachers and students. When the county would not provide a social studies teacher, he taught social studies.

Significant milestones:

An Electric Pump with 'Running' Water

Indoor Bathrooms: Mr. Hart and volunteers from the PTA and community built the facility and performed much of the work

Flavor Sidewalks Between Buildings
He did most of the work himself with help from the "big" boys

Established a Lunch Program
Each family was asked to donate a place setting or anything else they could "spare", (plate, knife, fork, spoon). Initially students stood up to eat. Mr. Hart and others soon built benches for students to sit.

Established a Football program, 1954-55
The uniforms were green and white because most of the uniforms and equipment came from Ocala High School where school colors were green and white. All the men on campus helped including the principal.

School Library
Bookshelves were installed in a classroom to house books. Many teachers contributed personal books and magazines to the 'Library'

Drivers Education
An Inverness teacher provided driver education two times per week

First Graduating Class, 1954

Junior/Senior Trips
Instead of a prom, Mr. Hart encouraged students to plan a major educational trip. The first trip was taken in 1958 when the class of 1957 sponsored Junior/Senior trip to Atlanta and to Washington, DC. Subsequent Junior/Senior trips were to Atlanta, Stone Mountain, Lookout Mountain in Tennessee, New Orleans, Louisiana and Mammoth Caverns in Kentucky

DAD, THE MAN, THE MYTH, THE LEGEND
C. LAWRENCE DESMORE

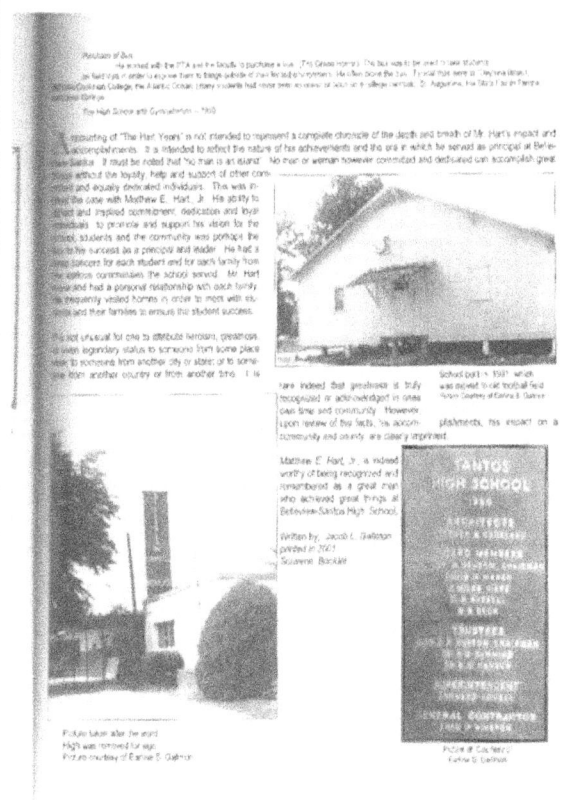

Reunion of Bus

He worked with the PTA and the faculty to purchase a bus. (The Graves money). The bus was to be used to take students on field trips in order to expose them to things outside of their familiar environment. He often drove the bus. Trips that were to Daytona Beach, Atlantic Oakbrook College, the Atlantic Ocean. Many students had never been exposed to such as a college campus, St. Augustine, the Ribs Florida Panhandle and Disneyland.

The High School and Gymnasium – 1950

The recounting of "The Hart Years" is not intended to represent a complete chronicle of the depth and breath of Mr. Hart's impact and his accomplishments. It is intended to reflect the nature of his achievements and the one in which he served as principal at Belleview–Santos. It must be noted that "no man is an island". No man or woman however committed and dedicated can accomplish great things without the loyalty, help and support of other committed and equally dedicated individuals. This was indeed the case with Matthew E. Hart, Jr. His ability to attract and inspired commitment, dedication and loyal individuals to promote and support his vision for the school, students and the community was perhaps the key to his success as a principal and leader. He had a high regard for each student and for each family from whom the school served. Mr. Hart knew and had a personal relationship with each family. He frequently visited homes in order to meet with students and their families to ensure that student success.

It is not unusual for one to attribute heroism, greatness or even legendary status to someone from some place else; to someone from another city or state; or to someone from another country or from another time. It is rare indeed that greatness is truly recognized or acknowledged in ones own time and community. However, upon review of the facts, his accomplishments, his impact on a community and country are clearly imprinted.

Matthew E. Hart, Jr. is indeed worthy of being recognized and remembered as a great man who achieved great things at Belleview-Santos High School.

Written by: Jacob L. Bateman
printed in 1993
Souvenir Booklet

Picture taken after the word
High was removed for sign.
Picture courtesy of Earline S. Gaitron

School built in 1937 which was adjacent to old football field
Picture Courtesy of Earline S. Gaitron

Picture of Cornerstone
Earline S. Gaitron

pg. 35

DAD, THE MAN, THE MYTH, THE LEGEND
C. LAWRENCE DESMORE

Souvenir Program
Of

BELLEVIEW-SANTOS HIGH

DEDICATORY SERVICES

NOVEMBER 11, 1956 — 3:30 P.M.
GYMNATORIUM

For the past seven years

that I have served as principal of this school, I have enjoyed the warm fellowship and fine cooperation of all members of our faculty, student body, and patrons. For all these, I am sincerely grateful.

The education and development of the whole child has always been our greatest concern at Belleview-Santos High. We shall continue to give each child those moral, spiritual, and educational values designed to equip him for life's responsibilities.

M. E. Hart, Jr., Principal

SPECIAL TEACHERS

Elementary Music .... Nookie Braxton
Speech Therapist .... Minnie Lamb
Visiting Teacher .... Gertrude V. Kirkland
Driver Education .... Reginald Packer
Supervisor of Negro Elementary Schools
Minnie Green

FACULTY ROSTER

Miss Thelma L. Brown	Grade 2
Mrs. Thelma T. Brown	Grade 3
Mr. J. B. Conway	Boy's Physical Educator
Mrs. Nakyolp Cushingham	Home Economics
Mr. Edmond Fordham	Soccer Station
Mrs. Annie C. Folton	Grade 3
Mrs. Ollie Gary	Grade 1
Mr. Emanuel M. Kinter	Agriculture
Miss Edda Miller	Girl's Physical Education
Mrs. Macie M. Montague	Mathematics
Mr. O. B. Sanders, Sr.	Science
Mrs. Rubye M. Snow	Grade 4
Miss Thelma Shalton	Business Education and English
Mrs. Thelma F. Weston	Grade 2 & 3

LUNCH PERSONNELL

Mrs. Irene Damon .... Manager
Mrs. Bertha Latti
Assistant to the luncheon
Priscilla Colton

(Information and copied from original Dedicatory Services Souvenir Program book)

DAD, THE MAN, THE MYTH, THE LEGEND
C. LAWRENCE DESMORE

Class of 1965

DAD, THE MAN, THE MYTH, THE LEGEND
C. LAWRENCE DESMORE

Class 1909 Back row Mr. Hart, W. Burlen, H. Brooks, S. Bothwell, D. Body, J. Hope, H. Damon, P. Godson, C. Howard, F. Hampton, J. Ponder, M. Hope, F. Wright, R. Gallmon, P. Hamilton, L. Johnson;
Seating M. Kendrick, B. King, N. Wallace, A. Fields, M. Samuel, C. cmes, V. Rich, C. Faison, M. Jay, E. Samuel, M. Rawls,
Seating on Floor L. Hope, T. Hector, S. Ellis

DAD, THE MAN, THE MYTH, THE LEGEND
C. LAWRENCE DESMORE

ROUND TWO OF THE LAST YEAR IN HIGH SCHOOL

I set my mind to graduate and get a scholarship in Music at a major school in Florida. In watching the news one evening plans were set to celebrate the first year of Dr. Martin Luther King, Jr. assassination, January 15, 1969, his birthday. When we raised the request for a program in SGA meeting it was blocked. Everyone knew I would do something but no one knew what. (I didn't know what I would do).

When I got off the bus, I walked to the flagpole, took my horn out the case and played taps while lowering the flag. The students gathered, we prayed and went to class. I was suspended for three days. I didn't argue because no one could understand how I felt about my blackness and Dr. King nor did they want to. Those days the black students would not speak except to acknowledge their name at roll call. I went home at the end of the day for a three-day break.

We had a basketball game on the night of

my second day home. The ten black players walked out that afternoon leaving only the two white players for the game. What I was told was the white players made the conference team and no blacks did. The coach and the assistant principal called me. They wanted to talk. I invited them to my house because I couldn't call the school, so I couldn't talk to anyone at school. They came to ask me to talk with the black players. I asked, "would the suspension end today?" Both said "yes". I called two players about the suspension ending and they voted to play. I went to the game.

That was the last time I was suspended but I continued the movement. However, the last two incidents involved the band director.

First, he called an unscheduled band practice that I did not attend. This forfeited my solo seat, and I was demoted to second seat. I was pissed! I don't play second. I noticed the school had a French horn that no one played, so I retired my Cornet.

The bad news was first my lip got too large and I couldn't play my Cornet unless I went to a larger mouthpiece. Second, the number of scholarships that I was offered were surprising. I only had two offers to black colleges and I was disappointed. I knew that the band director had not advocated for me the way he did his white students even though I was better that most of them. I guess he figured that if he couldn't get me one way he would find another way to disturb my progress. I often wondered would my life have been the same had I gone to college right out of high school? (Although I did graduate from one of those schools after serving in the Navy, with pride and I enjoyed every minute)

Two days after high school graduation my youngest sister was born, two months later we moved back home to Daytona Beach. (I preferred Daytona because it's on the mainland not the beach.)

DAD, THE MAN, THE MYTH, THE LEGEND
C. LAWRENCE DESMORE

I was still disappointed about the scholarships but I tried working the beach side restaurants and hotels. The last job I had before I entered the Navy, the hotel owner noticed two hotel guests (white females) and I were talking and later went out. When I returned to work on Monday, I received my W-2 form a handshake and a good luck. I had planned to quit the coming Friday anyway. I was leaving for the Navy on Good Friday, March 26, 1970.

DAD, THE MAN, THE MYTH, THE LEGEND
C. LAWRENCE DESMORE

High School Band

DAD, THE MAN, THE MYTH, THE LEGEND
C. LAWRENCE DESMORE

DAD, THE MAN, THE MYTH, THE LEGEND
C. LAWRENCE DESMORE

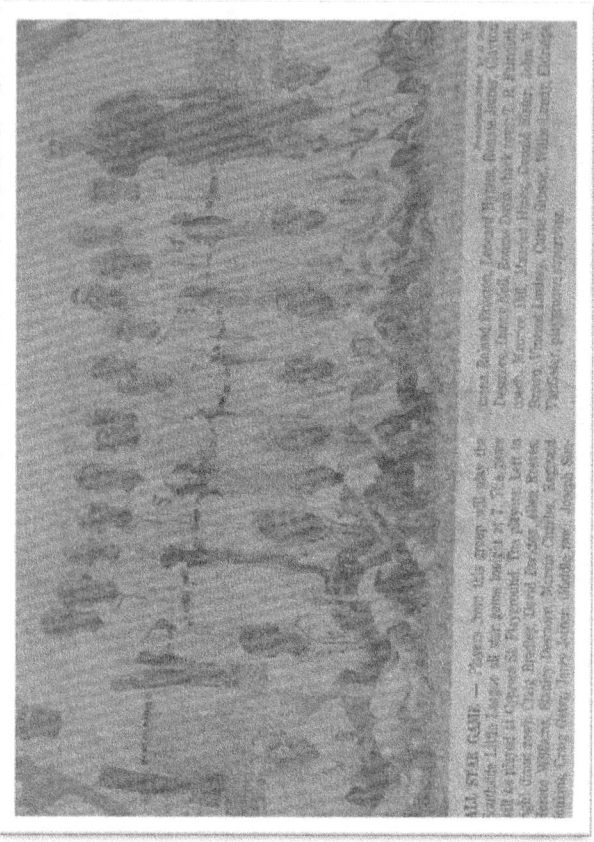

THE FIRST TIME IN THE NAVY

DAD, THE MAN, THE MYTH, THE LEGEND
C. LAWRENCE DESMORE

Navy Boot Camp Class of 1970

Often African-Americans have something
to say about the military, well,
I'm going to clear some thoughts.

Many ask, "Why should an African-American fight for a country that don't care about them"? My response usually is "do you care about you"? The military must be used as a bridge between childhood to adulthood in training the youth for a usable skill, once they leave the military." In my case, I wanted to be an auto mechanic in the Army however; my test scores were high enough to be a clerk in the Navy, which was suggested the Army recruiter.

Sure, I thought about the ocean and all that water. Well, *I can't swim*. The offer was good, two years of active, four years of reserves, three hot meals a day, showers, a bed and a pay check. This sounded great. Wrong. I had no plan.

My only plan was go for the shortest time possible. I believe that if I'm going to put my life on the line, I 'm going to get something back. In talking with my Dad about the Navy from his Navy experience, he didn't say too much. Once he said that the African- American assignments were limited to cooking, cleaning the ship and doing laundry.

Being the man that I am, I was not going to do that, so on my paperwork entering I checked the race box black, but when I arrived at the Recruit Training Center in Orlando, Florida, I checked the race box white because as an American wanting to serve my country my race should be of least importance.

I did have some good responsible duties in Recruit training, but I don't think race played a part except once. I was asked to carry my company's flag (058) and the Commander thought I was white. Well, I laughed because I thought it was my marching skills. (I knew that he might have seen somewhere that I was white). After eleven weeks of training I was ready to leave but I was having problems with floating in that pool the required distance, I almost didn't make graduation it with my company. Two weeks home then the adventure began.

Father's Day, June 16, 1970

The ship was in dry dock, it was dirty, low lightening and scary looking. I walked back to the phone booth at the end of the pier and called my Dad. I asked him to get me out of this and he said he couldn't. I wanted to cry but I said, "well" the Navy has 730 days to kill me and that was not going to happen.

I went aboard and stored my gear and made a two-year calendar. One of the first people I met on the ship was a sailor about my height, who lived in Florida. He was a boiler man second class. He talked me into becoming a boiler man. See, **no plan**. All I was thinking was that this sailor had six years in the Navy; it didn't hurt or kill him.
A boiler man had the dirtiest, hottest and dumpiest job. This was a job someone from Florida (or chose to live in Florida) would never want. The only civilian job in Florida for a boiler man is a firefighter.

My biggest reason for joining the Navy was to travel to places that I had read about in school. Places, such as - Spain, Italy, France, Greece and

DAD, THE MAN, THE MYTH, THE LEGEND
C. LAWRENCE DESMORE

Turkey. I could see the world. I did not mind any kind of job to see Cuba, and the Islands. Man, it was great, getting paid and having fun enjoying the journey; the water (ocean) never crossed my mind, except in stormy weather. With all the traveling, I lost track of time. After 3(six months) tours of Europe it was time to re-up (re-enlist) or go home. I was having fun, but I came home. Happy in serving my country, seeing the world, I had saved some money and still was not ready for college.

After my first two years in the Navy, things at home were still the same. I had some experience but nothing that I really wanted, as I mentioned earlier about the opportunity of a fireman. There was one African-American fireman in Daytona and he worked at the airport. The only boilers in Daytona were at the (Halifax) hospital. This was 1971 in Daytona Beach, Florida.

I tried working again, pumping gas, turning burgers and that wasn't working for me, so with a four-year obligation in the Navy Reserves, I decided that I should go back for two more years to complete my four-year obligation and see some more of the world, hopefully the Western side. I made E-4 in the Reserves that summer. I flew to Spain for my two weeks training to bring a ship back. The salty sea air had once again overpowered my will to stay on land.

I had met a "Mrs. Jones" that caught my interest and we had beautiful times together, so much so that I was becoming a parent for the first time. Her husband had seven brothers, I only had my brother and we couldn't fight that many guys at one time and win.

Having asked for the nearest duty station to Daytona because my sisters were entering their teen years and my brother away in college, I figured my mom needed me near home now. The Navy said welcome aboard once again. I was sent to Charleston, South Carolina assigned to a destroyer (great because I was experienced with them) headed for Vietnam.

THE VIETNAM WAR

"I know you might think of war as being exciting", my mom said, "but if something happened to you or your brother I would go crazy". Months before I went back to the Navy, I learned some of my friends in Ocala were killed or wounded for life and the thing that excited me about going to Viet Nam was really to **stop it, stop the war.**

This time in the Navy was fun; I knew what was expected of me. I don't remember the exact day I left for Charleston to meet my new shipmates, but I was on ship three days before we were headed to Viet Nam. My new CPO (Chief Petty Officer) and First Class Boiler man were African-American and that was great. Our first stop was Hawaii. It was nicknamed Paradise because it is a beautiful state. I always knew I was lucky, but as luck would have it my old ship anchored next to my new ship. It was great seeing old friends. On the trip, the CPO and 1st Class Boiler man checked my skills at sea working the boilers and decided to give me no duty in Hawaii. I was king of boilers on destroyers and my guys under my supervision were dukes, kings in the making.

See, I believe in safety first because I worked ten feet under the waterline in steam with about 3 1/2 inches of steel between the ocean and me. Safety is so important because if that super- heated boiler meets that cold ocean water, steam would form and chock your lungs to death. The other important thing was to teach my guys how to work smart, do one thing while thinking on the next task.

In Hawaii, when the gangplank dropped to go ashore, I checked this beautiful place out. After playing tourist by day and clubs by night, remember this was 1972. My Daddy had earlier told me to be careful there, but the people were friendlier than any country in Europe, but oh it is one of the fifty states. I love Hawaii.

The last night there, I met a wonderful young lady. I hadn't given much on relationships. As we were preparing to castoff she called me to get my address. She wrote me almost every day, if it was a holiday, even the little ones, she would send me a care package (baked goods, peanuts, candies). I started writing her and keeping a diary. As we continued writing I would tell her where I was going and she would make my hotel reservations, tell me where to eat and what to order. The waitress would ask "what's your name", and when I told her, she'd make a phone call, minutes later a car would arrive with very beautiful young ladies waiting to take me to my hotel. (This happened about four times in China, Japan). I was scared at first be- cause the hotel was raided, every room on my floor was opened except my room, so I asked why and she said, "they know who is in this room and no illegal activities were taking place" and that was her uncle heading the raid. For someone to have done this for me, she had to be special. I also learned that she'd sent my mother some flowers and called to introduce herself.

The writing continued as I went west to Subic Bay of the Philippines Islands. There, I basically lived on shore in an apartment and when I had to work a friend would keep my place. This experience was very rewarding. I never would have enough money to afford all this traveling, but those that didn't return home, the price was too great.

The war ended and my ship was the last to leave, coming through the channel locks of the Panama Canal surrounded by the "Virgin Forest' with some of the most beautiful birds I have ever seen. I know you'll not believe this but I've seen some wild natives as we passed through. Homeward bound. One stop left in Hawaii and to hopefully spend some time with my friend. In my letters, I had mentioned what to wear so I could identify her. Seven months away I wanted to know this special lady.

Remember me mentioning my work crew? One of the younger African- American sailors did not want to follow orders (he had caused problems on three other ships) and I was determined he was not going to make me lose my job. So, I had to let him go.

This was the hardest thing I had ever done at that point because he had no reason for what he was doing. He was doing just what they wanted him to do. Have another African-American write him up. I explained to him his choices. Why did he spend all this time in the Navy and throw it away with about one year to go? He did not care. Well, that day a helicopter carried him away and for a long time I thought about what he would tell his parents or when he'd realized he blew all his V.A. benefits. Well, I learned later that was exactly what he wanted. However, the CPO knew I did not want to do it to the brother, but I had to. When I explained my thoughts to the CPO, the question was, am I ready for my responsibilities?

At this time, I was studying for the second-class E-5 petty officer test, but in my mind evaluating his question. He once told me that the Navy was his father and mother, when it was only a job for me, and anyone that thinks different should not enlist. He had such a bad childhood his parents were separated and neither wanted him, but that was uncalled for.

We arrived in Hawaii and the piers were filled with people. One would think we were in Charleston, S.C. I spotted my friend before we docked. She was wearing a long black leather coat, high boots and nothing else, I was too excited. The knot headed CPO found me and said, "you can't leave the ship, you have duty." I tried to pay one of my shipmates to take my duty but he said, "I couldn't leave the ship." Knowing about my friend, he was being a jackass and it *pissed me off*. From that experience with him, I lost all respect for him as a man, not as a sailor.

Well, that made our relationship suffer even more. We were very happy to be home. Many of us had tailored made clothes from our Afros to stack shoes. I often thought of my Hawaiian friend. I was eager to call as soon as we docked. It wasn't that easy coming home after the Viet Nam War. We knew the politics behind it, but we went to do a job. As we approached the pier, we could see people gathering with banners, and welcome home signs, but we weren't allowed to dock until dark.

After securing the ship the non- duty sailors could go on leave for up to two weeks. On the way to get my car out of storage, near the airport, I tried to make conversation with the cab driver by mentioning I had just gotten back from the **NAM,** he stopped the car (three miles from the garage) turned around looked me eye to eye and said, "get out of the car, you baby killer." I was shocked. Boy, what a hero's welcome, and for the African-Americans that went it was an honor to have served but, reality hit and now there's two strikes against us. Don't get this wrong, for a long time I told my sons they didn't have to serve, I did it for every black man in this country.

After arriving home I wanted to stay

because there was so much going in the "super fly era" and the time had come for me to decide whether to re- enlist or get out. I had about 10 months on my contract when I met your mother. After that, the dream of my Hawaiian friend had all but died, and it was a difficult time. That problem I had with "Mrs. Jones", before I went in the Navy the second time, led her to tell me "if I married my friend from Hawaii I would **never see** my son" and I felt that we (African-Americans) were having enough problems. To bring in mixing of the races would have been the worst thing, I thought. Nevertheless, that's what happened. Sometimes, thinking about the past is dangerous. I would like to thank my Hawaiian friend and wish her well.

    The time had come for me to go back to work. A few months had passed and we received orders for the Med Cruise (back to Europe). I didn't like that, and my luck struck again, the orders were changed to South America. This is where I really wanted to go.

DAD, THE MAN, THE MYTH, THE LEGEND
C. LAWRENCE DESMORE

A friend told me that the ladies are prettier as you go from East around to West. I didn't believe him, he was right. I had about two months left but I wanted to go. First stops were Columbia, Venezuela and Brazil. Then it was time for me to come home. The women were beautiful, I stayed in Brazil six days, and it was great. I was a tourist once again. In my flight home stops were made in Bolivia, Ecuador and Peru. I must say it's a toss-up between Brazil and Peru on which country has the prettiest ladies. I had said good-bye to all my shipmates earlier before returning to Orlando where it all started. The only thing I had to do was process out. That took about four days. The Navy made me an offer, a bonus of $17,000 to stay in; I turned it down, because I was coming home for good. Sons, I knew then that the Navy was not to be my career. I told my Dad after completing high school; I would know what I wanted to do as a career in six years. Well, the military was ruled out. My last day was September 12, 1974. My discharge date, was one week after registration ended for the fall semester so I had to wait until the winter semester in January.

This gave me some time to adjust to being home. Your mom Sheryl and I decided to get married in December 1974, before Nicky first birthday on January the 23rd and school started on January 5th. Sheryl's parents wanted to adopt Nicky but I wasn't hearing it (remember my vow to me). Sheryl really wanted to get away from her parents' house, I explain to her that Nicky would be with me and that is that. The wedding took place and her Dad and I had so much partying he thought he was a chicken. But a few days passed and they were back to hating me again.

DAD, THE MAN, THE MYTH, THE LEGEND
C. LAWRENCE DESMORE

U.S.S. RICH (DD-820)
FLEET POST OFFICE
NEW YORK 09501

DD820/DRB:hs
1650
Ser: 222
28 May 1971

From: Commanding Officer, USS RICH (DD 820)
To: FN Clayton L. DESMORE, USN, B37 09 04

Subj: Letter of Appreciation

1. Your hard work and diligent efforts immediately preceeding deployment were such as to be worthy of special attention. Your willingness to sacrifice your normal liberty time to work long hours contributed significantly to RICH's readiness to make a distant deployment. Your cheerful efforts and professional ability are factors which have made possible RICH's high performance as a unit of the United States Sixth Fleet.

2. In recognition of your relentless efforts, the Commanding Officer takes great pride and pleasure in presenting you with this letter of appreciation for a job well done.

M. F. HANEHAN

Copy to:
BUPERS
Service Record

DAD, THE MAN, THE MYTH, THE LEGEND
C. LAWRENCE DESMORE

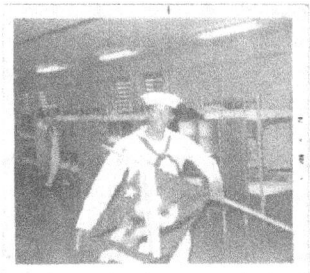

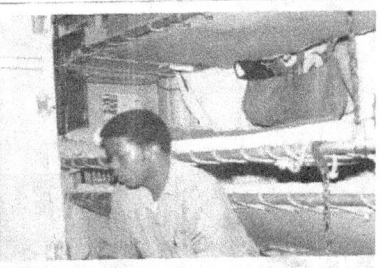

Navy Boot Camp

Ecclesiastes 3 King James Version (KJV)

3 To everything there is a season, and a time to every purpose under the heaven:
² A time to be born, and a time to die; a time to plant, and a time to pluck up that which is planted;
³ A time to kill, and a time to heal; a time to break down, and a time to build up;
⁴ A time to weep, and a time to laugh; a time to mourn, and a time to dance;
⁵ A time to cast away stones, and a time to gather stones together; a time to embrace, and a time to refrain from embracing;
⁶ A time to get, and a time to lose; a time to keep, and a time to cast away;
⁷ A time to rend, and a time to sew; a time to keep silence, and a time to speak;
⁸ A time to love, and a time to hate; a time of war, and a time of peace.
⁹ What profit hath he that worketh in that

wherein he laboureth?

10 I have seen the travail, which God hath given to the sons of men to be exercised in it.

11 He hath made everything beautiful in his time: also, he hath set the world in their heart, so that no man can find out the work that God maketh from the beginning to the end.

12 I know that there is no good in them, but for a man to rejoice, and to do good in his life.

13 And also that every man should eat and drink, and enjoy the good of all his labour, it is the gift of God.

14 I know that, whatsoever God doeth, it shall be forever: nothing can be put to it, nor any thing taken from it: and God doeth it, that men should fear before him.

15 That which hath been is now; and that which is to be hath already been; and God requireth that which is past.

DAD, THE MAN, THE MYTH, THE LEGEND
C. LAWRENCE DESMORE

Life at DBCC
Daytona Beach Community College

Classes started and I was ready. In my second semester, I learn about work-study program were students worked for the college and got paid. I came in as a Veteran work-study student in the registrar' office. I knew that catalog back to front and front to back. Students would come to me and ask questions all day long because they knew I was a student and not a part of the establishment.

The staff was quite surprised at how seriously I was into what I was assigned. Answering questions was what I did and I did it well. A year later, I was to graduate and I wanted to attend UCF (University of Central Florida). But knowing that Sheryl and I were having problems that were challenging for her I decided to go down the street to Bethune-Cookman College (B-CC), my first love.

Naturally it was their band that drew me; The Marching Men of Bethune Cookman! Let me also remind you, Sheryl had just left her parent's house and I'd been out in the world for a while so I understood what was happening and I didn't like it. She wanted her freedom and I wanted Nicky.

How many times have I said to you that, when the time comes and you have questions about the divorce you can read the records for yourself? I was hired by DBCC in July 1977 and I only needed one class to graduate, (remember earlier I mentioned a subject that I had always had problems with, *science*).

In my job interview, two questions were asked,

1. What can we do to better serve our students? My answer was that I would have an *orientation* for all first semester students.

2. Can you develop one for us? My response...YES, I CAN. I didn't know until later that the Presidential candidate from Georgia, son of a peanut farmer, had visited the campus and advised our President that the Blacks were not represented well in responsible areas (behind desk). If you had a degree, wanted to

work, and you happened to be Black, DBCC was the place. At that time, they were hiring like they were making a Tarzan movie.

I started getting that orientation together and in the spring term we tried our first run. There were some mistakes which I expected but I knew it would be ready for fall. Some of my co-workers did not like the idea because it was my idea and they were not going to support it until I got the administration to speak up for it. Everyone was advising counseling "one-on-one", but groups would save time, and reduce stress.

It was such a hit; it was my baby for *fourteen years*, from a one-projector slideshow, to a two-projector slideshow with a dissolve unit, to VHS tape, and one year away from viewing it at home on the college channel. On top of keeping this together with semester reports I still advised returning students for classes, clubs on campus, was a member of the State Board of Advisors for the Florida African-

American Student Association, and was promoted twice in one year. This was getting to be exciting.

Our first visit to the state conference for the Florida African- American Student Association was at the University of Florida in Gainesville. The college was gracious and paid for our rooms and meals. I really wanted this trip for two reasons: first, I wanted the students to see that the students at other schools were no different from them, and second, I wanted the Administration to realize that to make a wise investment in them was worth it.

During those days FAASA, Friday night opening speech contest, and I was coming to collect some hardware (trophies). We arrived about noon, checked in and met in my room. Some of my students didn't understand that meeting when other students were having fun playing in the pool just having fun. I explained to them that we will have fun after we get the hardware. So, we recorded their practice to have them ready for that evening. I had talked with a few advisers over the phone to let them know that I have students there to compete.

We all were invisible until that opening speech contest. My students won eight out of ten contests, they knew us then, and Daytona Beach Community College was in the house. At that moment, I knew that as long as I was there, DBCC would always be in the state conference. On Saturday, the winners were up early to attend classes and made new friends, I was so proud of them and over the years, many of our students held state officers with FAASA, and graduated from four year Colleges and Universities because of their FAASA experience.

The students talked about that trip so long we didn't have a problem recruiting students for the club anymore. The administration was proud to because they could call their friends at the schools and brag about our proud weekend.

Registration took up seventy to eighty

percent of our time; it was nothing to have 2100 to 2500 new and transfer students in the fall and 1900 to 2100 in the spring, plus the returning student population and a staff of 8 to 12 to service them. And that's just the A.A. and A.S. degree programs.

It was a spring registration a few days before the semester started that I met Cathy. I was "burned out". I remember asking her "What have you been doing to register this late" she replied, "she was thinking about going to another community college" I said with confidence "then you would have missed meeting your husband". I could see the fear in her eyes but I saw a fearful young lady (ten years my junior) that the world was waiting on, and I needed to help her as well get you guys a "mom". I double- checked the "rules" about staff dating students to make her comfortable with me.

Her mother liked me in the early days of our relationship because she was working hard on her studies. She would go to our home and study and wait for you guys to get home from school and complete your homework before I got home from work. You all had that bond that I wanted so bad to see because if it didn't work out, I would not have asked her to marry me.

Those weekends when you and Nicky would visit Sheryl you did not want to go. I did not want to send you but the court said I was required to let you go. One of my reasons I did not like those visits was because Monday morning I would have to visit Nicky's school because he was restless and had not been taking his medicine at the right times. It became a problem for me at work so I started taking Mondays off until I could get the judge to understand what we were going through. Sheryl never paid child support so I asked (the judge) had it been me not paying child support what would happen to me, he ended the court ordered visits. Cathy said she had asked Sheryl to come to the house and visit but she never did.

Cathy was great for us; our biggest problem was she wanted to have children and I stopped that after you were born. I had a nightmare of having a house full of children and no help.

Even with this problem, we got married but the feeling of having children never left her mind. One time, I thought of going to St. Louis to have a reversal, but that nightmare of children and no help would not leave me alone.

We divorced, but we will always be friends. She met a guy and they have two sons that are giving her "hell", but she's all right. Occasionally, I see her in the store and we talk about the old days.

I needed to thank her for helping us. I did not have to but parents living with married children can be difficult. I asked her many years later, what she thought was our problem, she said "her friends were telling her that I wanted to be with someone else". Many times, friends don't want to see you doing the right things to achieve a goal and will put things in your head to stop you.

My number one goal was **you guys** and when my job at DBCC stopped being *fun* I knew I would leave.

I was doing too much with projects on the job, student activities, the family time, my health; everything was running into each other. I reduced my work by getting off campus and visiting other interesting areas. I developed a plan of visiting high schools in remote areas of the county to test seniors and to save them traveling to the campus to be admitted. I wanted them to know that we had something for everyone.

During this stage, there was no campus with our college name out there. I was scheduled to visit a high school one morning and the car I was to use was not clean. I got into a "back and forth" with the guy who was supposed to clean the car because I decided that I was representing the college and I should travel like the President of the college. I was not going in a dirty car, so I walked back to my office to call the school and tell them I was not coming.

By the time, I arrived at my office, my vice president called me in his office. We talked and I explained the problem. The phone rang, he answered, turned to me and said the car is ready, are you going? I said, "yes and by the way I need you to buy me a briefcase because this box doesn't look professional". Shaking his head, he said, "okay, it will be in your office when you return."

People will never know what's on your mind, if you don't speak up. The man responsible for having the cars clean was my "buddy", Fred's supervisor. He spoke to Fred, "you know your "buddy" is a trouble-maker."
One of my get-a-ways took me to an interesting place called **prison.** *This is a reaction story about my time in prison.*

DAD, THE MAN, THE MYTH, THE LEGEND
C. LAWRENCE DESMORE

THE GATES

I personally hate the system of "corrections" because it has become a system of warehousing. There are no adjustments for their return to society. All Human Beings need to feel responsible for our society. I asked for a visit to the prison before the test date to get a conception of a prison. The request was granted.

The person I was to see met me in the parking lot. He was returning to the compound in a truck with caged dogs from an attempted escape. "Whew", that was something; we entered the compound through two barbed wire gates. The first gate closed with aloud hollowness. Suddenly, I felt out of character, like my life was as temporary as a young bird that had fallen from his nest. I held my breath and continued to walk. The second gate closed and I felt death was one step away.

After being inspected, we went to a trailer in the middle of the compound to meet Ms. Farmer who was to show me the testing location. As I waited for Ms. Farmer to finish what she was doing, I noticed that the inmates (I preferred to call them "time residents") would enter asking for a pencil, another entered asking for a piece of chalk, another entered asking for an aspirin. Once alone, "I asked curiously, what is going on?" The reply was," you are new to this community. They want to know who you are and what your business here is".

    I knew I would be leaving but the "time residents" certainly did not make the visit friendly at this point. Ms. Farmer and I began the walk across the Compound, passing three "time residents". One of the ones that she knew, refused to let her pass. She asked him if he wanted to add six months to his time, he answered "no" and moved. It amazed me that time can be added that simply. We finally reached the area where the test would take place. The Administration building, the one where I was inspected upon arrival. As we walked and talked, I learned that the prison housed minimum risk "time residents," I later learned that there were many exceptions. She also mentioned that the testing could only happen at night, "oh h_ _ _ no". My mind started racing, the test time is three hours, fifteen minutes to setup the room, fifteen minutes to wrap up and clear the room, thirty minutes to drive there, thirty back on that dirt road. No lights, oh well, I should get home about 12:00 midnight.

I arrived about 6:10 p.m., the gate did not sound as bad as before but I was not, and am still not, accustomed to the idea of not coming and going as I please. I set up the room for forty-five, opened the doors to let them in about 6:50 p.m. I began my opening introduction by telling a few "ice breakers". I remembered to tell them who I was and what business I had there, and "I am a friend to you all". After a few minutes, they were laughing, now I can relax.

Looking over the group I noticed one seat empty, but it was time for the test to begin. After reading the instructions, I asked if there were any questions, there were no response, so, I set the clock and they began testing. I explained to them that they could not fail the test and most were very relieved. I tried to be as invisible as possible usually thumbing through a magazine, or walking around the back of the room. I spent most of the time observing them from the back of the room. One "late time resident" entered looking upset, I asked if he wanted to test, he said "yes". I whispered, "Read the instructions and when you're finished raise your right hand. If you have any questions raise your left hand. He took a letter out of his back pocket and threw it to the floor missing the trashcan. I asked the guard what that was about. This young man **could not** obtain a mistrial hearing on a murder charge. Imagine being eighteen years old and looking at life in a prison. Nevertheless, he continued the test.

In my observation of testing "time residents", I noted that they grouped themselves in three communities. One group dressed in flip-flops or tennis shoes, red or blue handkerchiefs on their heads, and lots of pleats in the back of their shirts. Another group dressed I would say "normal", but the third group's clothes were wrinkled as if they didn't care. I learned after a discussion with the guards that group one (or the flip flop and handkerchiefs) was homosexuals: group two (the normal) was too due to be released soon and group three the "I don't care crew" were Lifers.

Testing was complete about 10:45 p.m.; I collected every pencil, booklet, and scrape paper as they returned to their cells. Man, I was excited it was over, with time to spare. The process of leaving is the same as entering but in reverse order: first the inspection and embarrassing moment, then "the gates". I dance to the "gates" and they opened **_gate one_**, it had a joyous sound of near freedom, then **_gate two_** opened, I was so relieved I could have kissed the ground.

I stood in the parking lot silently waiting for "the gates" to close and, for some reason; it did not sound that loud after all. As I drove into the night my thoughts were to never enter "the gates: again. Well, I have been back on programs four or five times. I don't like the prison system, but someone had to try to make a difference.

This experience made me think, that prison with mostly filled with men who looked like me so, this led me to write a program for young men in high school, working on their GED, or in detention centers. I titled it, "Save <u>O</u>ur <u>S</u>ons" that grew to "Save Our Children". I tell them how my life went "From a Mess to a Miracle," and gave them hope with exercises to help- themselves.

DAD, THE MAN, THE MYTH, THE LEGEND
C. LAWRENCE DESMORE

We're Here... Where Are You?

CLAYTON L. DESMORE, SR. is a counselor and academic advisor. The 1985 Bethune-Cookman College graduate provides students with program and course information. He is also the administrator of the new student orientation program where he develops and directs slide shows and video tapes, schedules orientation sessions, and coordinates personnel work schedules. A Navy veteran, Desmore was voted one of the Outstanding Young Men of America in 1982. He is married and has two sons. His interests include racquetball, scouts and traveling.

Clayton L. Desmore, Sr.

There's A Place for You
at
Daytona Beach Community College
It's An Equal Opportunity Institution
For More Information, Phone 254-3020

This article appeared in the Daytona Times March 13-19, 1986.

Clay Desmore
9/1/86

YEARS LATER

DAD, THE MAN, THE MYTH, THE LEGEND
C. LAWRENCE DESMORE

December 5, 1995, Corey went into the Navy; the letter that you read earlier is the letter he gave me leaving home for the first time. Boys have a struggle with coming home harder than girls; they usually bring a girlfriend and hopefully a wife home to visit. Well, Corey has this thing about older women to; (I saw too much of me in him and it wasn't pleasant) therefore I suggested go to school or the service and grow up. A couple years later Corey met and married (an older woman) and they give me my first grandson, born October 23, 1999.

Nicky was having a hard time understanding where Corey was but over time he adjusted. Nicky turn twenty-two so the last six months of school year and he was in "home school". I felt it was unfair but he seemed <u>tired</u> of going too regular school. The lady that kept him had a fish tank at her home; so, I purchased one and let them fix it up at our home. Two month later, Nicky's placement for a group home in Port Orange was ready. I really didn't want him in a group home but I had to work. If I had known that he could have gotten a Social Security or possibly a VA check at birth because of my Viet Nam experience, I (probably) would kept him home, but I didn't know. I wanted him to have the experience of being an adult.

LEAVING DBCC

DAD, THE MAN, THE MYTH, THE LEGEND
C. LAWRENCE DESMORE

One Sunday in church January 1997, I prayed to leave DBCC (now Daytona State College) somehow and I heard a voice ordering me to "come to this place in the church" I went and prayed some more, and then the voice said, "Build a grocery store in the black community". A few months went by and DBCC started downsizing. Anyone with 10 years or more could retire and receive a check for eight years. I couldn't leave on the first date (November 97), but could on the second dated (June 98), I found out that I had a year of vacation leave I could take, so I took a two-month vacation, and went back to work only to check out. I'm blessed and Thankful. If this had not happened I probably would be at DBCC today, God is Great.

I felt like a "freed slave". I had talked with Nicky and Corey about this plan and how the job was affecting my health. Yes, I will to leave them something, but I was not going to kill myself trying to do it? God will make a way.

The first three months with no income was the

pits. Then the job that was promised by The Department of Juvenile Justice fell through because of the elections and the person that was to hire me was fired. I worked on public speaking and a self- help program for teens in the DJJ system and people working on their GED (General Education Degree) that felt left out. I got a food stamp card because, how can I tell others about this experience unless I went through it. The first thing the unemployment lady told me was that I should get a job teaching because "I write very well". I laughed and told her I just left that career after 21 years, thanks but no thanks. I went to the Salvation Army to get some "emergency food," I didn't need it because I have my Mom and four sisters in this town, but community services experience was useful.

    I figured, I better try and work a few more years and retire for real. I was a night custodian part time at Palm Terrace Elementary School from November to August. My supervisor always asked me "what is a man with a degree and 21 years of experience in advising looking for?" My reply was "I am waiting for the Bus".

A Spruce Creek High School campus advisor job opened, I applied and got it, therefore the Bus had come. I had to ask someone what is a campus advisor in a High School? I was at the "Creek" for one full year and started the second but was not doing what was promised "mentoring". Before I left Palm Elementary, I re-met Lucy, in church. We met previously at Bethune-Cookman College in 1982. Lucy was in real estate and later a teacher in Sanford about the time I started working at the Department of Children and Family Services in the foster care unit.

At Children and Family Services, I thought my job was people helping people that wanted to better themselves. I thought I might be able to help these families in crisis. I did not know how BAD the crisis with families had gotten. Most parents were involved with a drug called *crack.* My focus was so wrong.

Lucy and I dated a while, but after fourteen years of being single I wanted a wife, someone that was a friend, without young children, and with similar beliefs in God and a strong work ethic. I also wanted someone who wanted to enjoy life (without the drama of children). That voice about a grocery store in the neighborhood was still there but I didn't see it.

DAD, THE MAN, THE MYTH, THE LEGEND
C. LAWRENCE DESMORE

THE 2002 YEAR

Most years start with January but June 2002 started my test of will. I asked Lucy to marry me and she chose to have a June wedding. That was fine with me because it didn't interfere with sporting events in the Fall, like football. We knew that the DCF job was to end June 30, 2002 but that's okay.

Look at this real close... we got married on June the 8th, 2002. It was a beautiful morning wedding everything was in place, we were nervous as hell, but wanted to do it. Lucy's mom is in her mid-eighties and I wanted her to see that I was for real and her only child was in good hands. Everyone was in place, Nicky was all dressed up but my Dad was missing. The wedding went on as planned and I was ready to celebrate my third wedding.

After cleaning the church, we rushed home to change clothes and begin our life as a married couple. As we are preparing to leave, a taxicab pulls up with my Dad. He said that he had something to do earlier and did not give the details. We thought it was kind of strange but anyway we were off to our honeymoon.

We were gone on our honeymoon for four days but on the eighth day of being married (Father's Day), I was at the computer typing thank you notes for gifts from the wedding before going to church. The phone rings and it was Nicky's group home. The person was crying and screaming. She was saying, "I can't wake him up". I thought it was a Father's Day joke and I asked who is this? The reply was, "Mr. Clay I can't wake Nicky up." My thoughts went numb, couldn't see, just blank. I asked her to take a few deep breaths, as I did and I said again, "tell me what you are saying clearly".

She repeated, "I can't wake Nicky up, he's dead". "Oh, my God, what am I to do now?" Lucy and my mom were at church singing in the choir. It was Father's Day and the family was there also. They knew I was coming to the next service, but I had to let someone know what I had just learned. It was a challenge to drive that mile and a half to the church, but Nicky was about thirty miles away and I knew that I was in no shape to drive that far to get to him. I almost passed out in the parking lot and asked someone to get Lucy and mom for me.

We returned home and the coroner's office called and said his death was natural, and if I wanted an autopsy the doctor would not sign the death certificate. What kind of person tells a grieving parent that kind of thing over the phone? I didn't know what to do? The Debary funeral home called and repeated what the Coroner's office said and that they would contact the local funeral home for pick up. I called my choice of funeral homes to get in touch with them. They asked me why I didn't have an autopsy done and I explained to them that as much medicine as Nicky was taking I was convinced that it was not needed. I was really in no shape to make that decision. I remembered, a doctor telling Sheryl and me early in his life that he may not live to be twenty; however, I was still in shock because he was dead.

The question of "What I should have" or "could have done" will be with me the rest of my life. Later that afternoon, I tried to contact Corey through the Red Cross because he was being stationed at a new post in a different state and they would locate him but his wife would have to make the request. (I thought that was strange, this is my son). I needed to let Sheryl know but she's was in the hospital on life support, so I called her sister to let them know and ask her not to tell Sheryl until tomorrow, it may be a better time for her. They waited, told her on Monday and she died that Tuesday night. Now, Corey's wife had to call him and tell him this news. Can you image that eight days after I get married, losing one of my sons on Father's Day, then two days later their mother dies?

I couldn't talk Sheryl's family into having one funeral service, so Sheryl's was in the morning and Nicky's was in the afternoon, it made the day very long and difficult, her father didn't attend Nicky's service but mentioned that when Nicky was a baby they wanted to adopt Nicky (go figure).

I went back to the Department of Children and Families to sign out that I would not be back. Remember, the job was over the end of June and this was the 18th. On Wednesday, the group homeowner and manager came to Daytona to bring their sorrows with a *blank check* to pay for everything, the service, his suit, casket, and offer to buy food or anything we may need. I was still numb times two now that Sheryl had passed. No amount of money would have replaced them I needed to do what I think Jesus would have wanted me to do. So, I let them pay for the service, casket, and the suit.

I called his caseworker and she could not talk with me about Nicky's passing. She said it was a department policy and she would be fired. **Nicky's death began to look like some people were hiding something from me**. In this short period of time I began to wonder why...

    1) the doctors, would not sign the death certificate if I'd ask for an autopsy,

    2) the coroner insisted it was a natural death,

    3) the owner offering to pay for everything,

    4) the caseworker actions,

    5) the group home is facing a fire station why did they call the hospital miles away,

    6) the group home staff was at the service and the young man that shared a room with Nicky was on the program, however, he had a look like he knows something and can't talk,

    7) it took about three months to get the police report. After I got the report I began to talk with some lawyers and one told me "this is another case of another

poor black man with no money". Now if you know me, you know I wanted to beat his ass. If someone would have taken the case the group homeowner would have been sued, along with and their employer, the state and his law firm.

I asked Lucy when summer school ended not to go back to teach in Sanford. I wanted her closer home. She got a job in Daytona and enjoyed it, however, it was quite stressful. Someone told us that if she stayed there two years, we would be divorced. She noticed the long hours and decided one year would be enough. I wasn't working, but one day she came home complaining about the hair store she had just left. This was not the first time I'd heard complaints from her about the hair stores so I asked her about having our own hair store. She asked me if I were kidding, I said no. So, she quit that job on a Friday and Monday we had a grand-opening of CLD Hair and Beauty Supply. Remember, I wanted a grocery with many small stores around it.

Funding could not be raised for the building so we decided to open the hair store. It was an experience I will never forget. After about nine months in the business we moved to a larger building with signs in the door of our new location and someone called and said how sorry they were to see that we were out of business but never came to the store.

NO ONE WILL BE HAPPY ABOUT **YOUR** SUCCESS EXCEPT YOU.

Your Grand-Daddy had moved back to Daytona from Jacksonville to be closer to us and in October he was killed crossing the street late one night. I'll never forget when the police and Chaplin called to let me know. We got dressed and went to mom's house, I was numb again. On our way there, I drove right past where he laid and told Lucy somebody's been hit, not realizing it was my Dad. At Mom's house, some of my sisters came and we prayed, and tried to think of what was needed. My mind was blank, three deaths in twenty months when before it was one every thirteen years was a bit overwhelming. I asked God again "what was going on" or once more "what had I done". The answer was "these three flowers you thought you would have to take care of all your life; I have them now. Enjoy your life and marriage".

The day the funeral home had Dad's viewing for the public, we had planned meeting with some investors about our grocery store and could not reschedule. Mom understood we had people coming to conduct business but I could feel the rest of my family thought I should cancel. They would have been at the funeral home about a 1½ hours without us, and I said this jokingly, "Dad wasn't going anywhere". At the meeting, we explained what we had to do so everyone stayed focused. We handled our business and still got there before the viewing was over.

HELLO DADDY

Remember I mentioned my reasons for re-entering the Navy and "Mrs. Jones" and I having a son, well she also had a daughter (possible by me) that was kept a secret. She died shortly after Mother's Day 2005.

I'd finished some work at the church and walked through the courtyard where the pastor's wife and a lady were setting. The pastor's wife left the lady sitting there in the prayer garden. At the service on Mother's Day the men conduct the worship service and provide dinner for the ladies. I had a serving tray of juices and a man I didn't know asked to help me. I thought he and the woman I had seen in the courtyard were married, so in my introduction to them, I stated my name and to "please tell your husband thanks for helping me serve the juice". She jumped up, loudly saying, "you them children Daddy?". I tried the get her to control herself and not be so loud. Then she said, "my husband died last year". I apologized and she said, "sit with me a minute". Of course, I didn't want to after getting busted, but, I wanted to know what she thought she knew about me. Well she knew "Mrs. Jones", the times and dates we were together and how we met.

I told her and baby girl, there was nothing we could do but continue to respect "Mrs. Jones'" husband. See, they had divorced years ago, and "Mr. Jones" married the lady that he was dating while I was dating is wife. I didn't mind the children that I did not raise calling me Daddy or visiting because I had been in a relationship with their mother.

Whenever she needed something she knew how to reach me. And she had reached out to me many times. I know I was *wrong* and very young but things do happen. Her husband and I have talked but never about her or the children because he knew how I felt, but nothing was going to change.

My reason for including this is because; I learned from this experience that if I father any other children I am going to be there for them.

That promise was made before Nicky or you were born and when your mother and I divorced you were 4 and Nicky was 6. That is why I fought so hard for custody. I can't say that their Daddy did not love them, but what I know for sure is I love all of you and all of you have made **me a better father and a better man.**

The beginning of 2008, I started looking at my health because there were several things going on. Lucy's mother had been living with us almost two years and I was **stressed out**. No one was expecting this or at least, *I was not expecting this*, but I agreed, as long as she would attend a day program for seniors. I worked at home most of the time and didn't need her help. She decided one day in May 08 that she was not going back to the program so she is now at an assisted living home because we can't leave her home by herself.

Lucy's stressed, I'm stressed, so something must change. I visited the VA clinic and started some tests, and they thought that I had (in 1997) or would be having a "heart attack" soon. I am now taking medicine, checking my blood pressure daily and trying not to be stressed. I have done what they told me except quit smoking. I did however, change to a lighter cigarette and cut back. I have not quit, yet. After some new test, my heart is in good shape; however, my lungs may have cancer from t h e hazards of my job in the Navy as a boiler man, working around asbestos.

Earlier in this journey I mentioned several times that I have my <u>fears</u> but, as a Christian, I am not going to let fear get the best of or affect my health by stressing me out. I'm going to go on about my day and think about my next day and perhaps the next book. I believe that the final say belongs to God almighty.

LAYING THE HEADSTONE

It has been fourteen years and nine months that this has been on my mind. I thought and thought, but there was NO time to decide the happenings, (what or when a thing can or should). Tonight, I received a message from a distance...the voice of God. "Whatever you do, share it with the group-home where Nicky's last breath was taken. It is time to Forgive, FORGIVE".

I have come to the under-standing that **God's plan is God's plan** and it is not possible to change it. The years, we shared with Nicky, will *NEVER BE FORGOTTEN, and TRUE LOVE lasts FOREVER.*

Whenever the time comes for the stone laying, I will invite the group-home to attend. Forgiveness is not just for the forgiven but also for the forgiver.

DAD, THE MAN, THE MYTH, THE LEGEND
C. LAWRENCE DESMORE

Clayton &
Sons
Corey and
Clay, Jr.
1992

Clayton L. Desmore's First birthday party

Do you see the cake in the left hand

DAD, THE MAN, THE MYTH, THE LEGEND
C. LAWRENCE DESMORE

Reva P. Desmore
Mom

Edward S. Desmore
Dad

DAD, THE MAN, THE MYTH, THE LEGEND
C. LAWRENCE DESMORE

Clayton L. Desmore
The author

DAD, THE MAN, THE MYTH, THE LEGEND
C. LAWRENCE DESMORE

Edward S. Desmore with
Clayton at the "Manner"
in uniform of the
Marching Men of Bethune-Cookman

DAD, THE MAN, THE MYTH, THE LEGEND
C. LAWRENCE DESMORE

We Miss You!
Clayton Lawrence Desmore, Jr.

Born
Jan 23, 1974

Went Home
June 16, 2002

AMEN!

www.ingramcontent.com/pod-product-compliance
Lightning Source LLC
Chambersburg PA
CBHW071522080526
44588CB00011B/1531